POEMS FOR
BIG
IMAGINATIONS

A BIG thanks to the Year 6 children and staff of Nightingale Primary School, Hackney, London, who, as part of a school project, followed the production of this book from first draft to publication. Here's what they said:

"Our school loves Neal Zetter poems and this new collection is sure to delight teachers and children alike." **Abigail Hopper, Headteacher**

"Neal's poems are inclusive, fun and engaging! Humour, word play, and a short format ensure that it is a book catered for all! It is always a pleasure to have Neal in our school and we all love working with him."
Shamim Patel, Class Teacher and Writing Lead

"Neal's poems spark smiles, laughter, and endless requests for more!"
Rachel Mills, Class Teacher

"A source of constant laughter and excitement in our classroom! I highly recommend to every class teacher across the country."
Esme Cargill, Class Teacher

"A whirlwind of emotions, just like a merry-go-round!"
Lennie

"His poems inspire me and make me want to ROAR with joy!"
Hannah

"His poems are so creative—you'll never find anything else like them."
Elifsu

"Neal's poems are wonderfully written and very entertaining."
Akira

"Neal's poems challenge me, but I enjoy figuring out the jokes."
Mustafa E

"An outstanding and unique book with a spark of pizzazz!"
Jean

"A book where you go up and down and swirl around."
Khyro

"This book is so amazing I wanted to keep on reading!"
Jeremiah

"A delightful book that blew my mind into a world of poems."
Akeela

"A book that takes you on a ride through imagination!"
Maya

"Every time I read Neal's poems, they always cheer me up."
Fadekemi

"These poems will forever hold a special place in my heart."
Jahrelle

"I've never seen a book like this – it's truly one of a kind!"
Shian

"Reading your poems makes me happy. How do they make you feel?"
Malachi

For all my fantastic family and friends – you know who you are – N.Z.

Emily, for all your help, especially with drawing pineapples – W.H.

Text copyright © Neal Zetter 2026
Illustrations Illustrations copyright © Will Hughes 2026

First published in Great Britain in 2026 by
Otter-Barry Books, Little Orchard, Burley Gate, Herefordshire, HR1 3QS
www.otterbarrybooks.com info@otterbarrybooks.com

All rights reserved
No part of this publication may be reproduced, stored in a retrieval system, or transmitted, in any form, or by any means, electrical, mechanical, photocopying, recording or otherwise without the prior written permission of the publisher or a licence permitting restricted copying. In the United Kingdom such licences are issued by the Copyright Licensing Agency (www.cla.co.uk).

A catalogue record for this book is available from the British Library.
Designed by Arianna Osti
ISBN 978-1-915659-87-3
Illustrated with line drawings
Printed in Great Britain
1 3 5 7 9 8 6 4 2

Authorised Representative: Easy Access System Europe
Mustamäe tee 50, 10621 Tallinn, Estonia, gpsr.requests@easproject.com

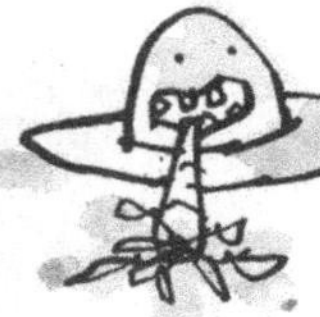

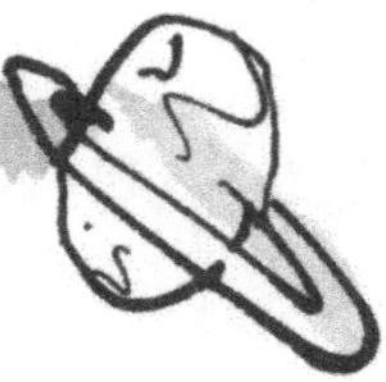

Small Poems for BIG Imaginations

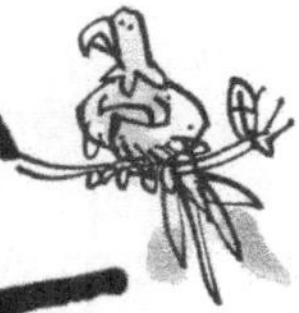

NEAL ZETTER

Illustrated by Will Hughes

Contents

Small	8
Longlegs	9
My Flabber	10
Fast	11
What to Wear?	12
Underground	14
It's OK to Fail	16
Book Meal	17
Chalk and Cheese	18
Oscillating Ocelot	20
Scrabble	21
Pockets	22
LostinSpace	23
Knock! Knock!	24
Rules?	26
Dissimiles	27
Dangerous Fruit	28
The Loooooooooongest Poem in the Universe	30
Friendship Formula	31
Chop	32
Limerick #1	33
Corners	34
oPOETician	36
Butterflies	37
Fearless	38
The Ghost Writer	40
Sleepy Dog	42
Lull	43

A Difficult Choice	44
Holes	46
K 8 a B	47
On Finding an Acorn	48
Limerick #2	50
Etc	51
Woodpecker, Woodpecker	52
Talk	54
Chopsticks	56
Pigs	57
Tiping	58
Shape Poem	59
Whodunnit?	60
Cupboard Under the Stairs	62
Birthday	64
Bugged	65
Henry's Wives	66
How Long is a Poem?	67
N Vwls	68
Fastly?	69
Magical	70
Brunch	72
Sky	74
Zzzzzzzz	76
Limerick #3	77
Sorted!	78
Finally?	79
About the Poet and the Illustrator	80

Small

Small poems are fabulous fun
So I thought I would write this one
It will not be too long I think
Cos my pen has run out of

Longlegs

I saw a daddy longlegs creeping 'cross a wall
I saw a daddy longlegs gliding down the hall
I saw a daddy longlegs lurking by your bed
I saw a daddy longlegs upside-down,
  quite dead

I saw a daddy longlegs running round the sink
I saw a daddy longlegs drowning in my drink
I saw a daddy longlegs crawling through
  a crack
I saw a daddy longlegs ready to attack

I saw a daddy longlegs underneath a rock
I saw a daddy longlegs chewing someone's
  sock
I saw a daddy longlegs sitting on the stair
But I've never seen a *mummy* longlegs
  anywhere!

My Flabber

My flabber is broken
My flabber is busted
Shredded! Shattered! Rotten! Rusted!

My flabber is mangled
My flabber is mashed up
Ravaged! Ruined! Crushed up! Smashed up!

It was a fine flabber
(At least, while it lasted)
And now it's destroyed
I'm left... flabbergasted!

Fast

My burger rushed and ran away,
my doughnut dashed and darted,
my chicken wings flew out the door,
my chips swiftly departed.
My pizza promptly disappeared,
too quick to be pursued.
So I then promised to myself,

"No more fast food!"

What to Wear?

I won't wear a wizard's outfit with a black
    moustache
Or a blonde wig as I'd look completely daft
Or a pirate's beard that's prickly and spiky
Or a leotard or a long white nightie

I won't wear the whiskers, tail and claws of a cat
Or a ten-gallon cowboy hat
Or a monster's suit with googly eyes
Or a cape (unless it helps me to fly)

I won't wear armour as it's sure to rust and
    creak
Or a clown's nose and big floppy feet
Or the costume of a giant bumblebee

Cos at your fancy dress party I'll be going as...

ME

Underground

I love the endless, snaking tunnels,
the noisy, rattling trains,
riding down the escalators,
then riding up again.

The odd assortment of passengers,
ads, posters and tube map,
the huge range of strange station names,
announcements like "MIND THE GAP!"

The robotic ticket barriers,
the queues, the crowds, the crush...
so can we please take the Underground
instead of the car or the bus?

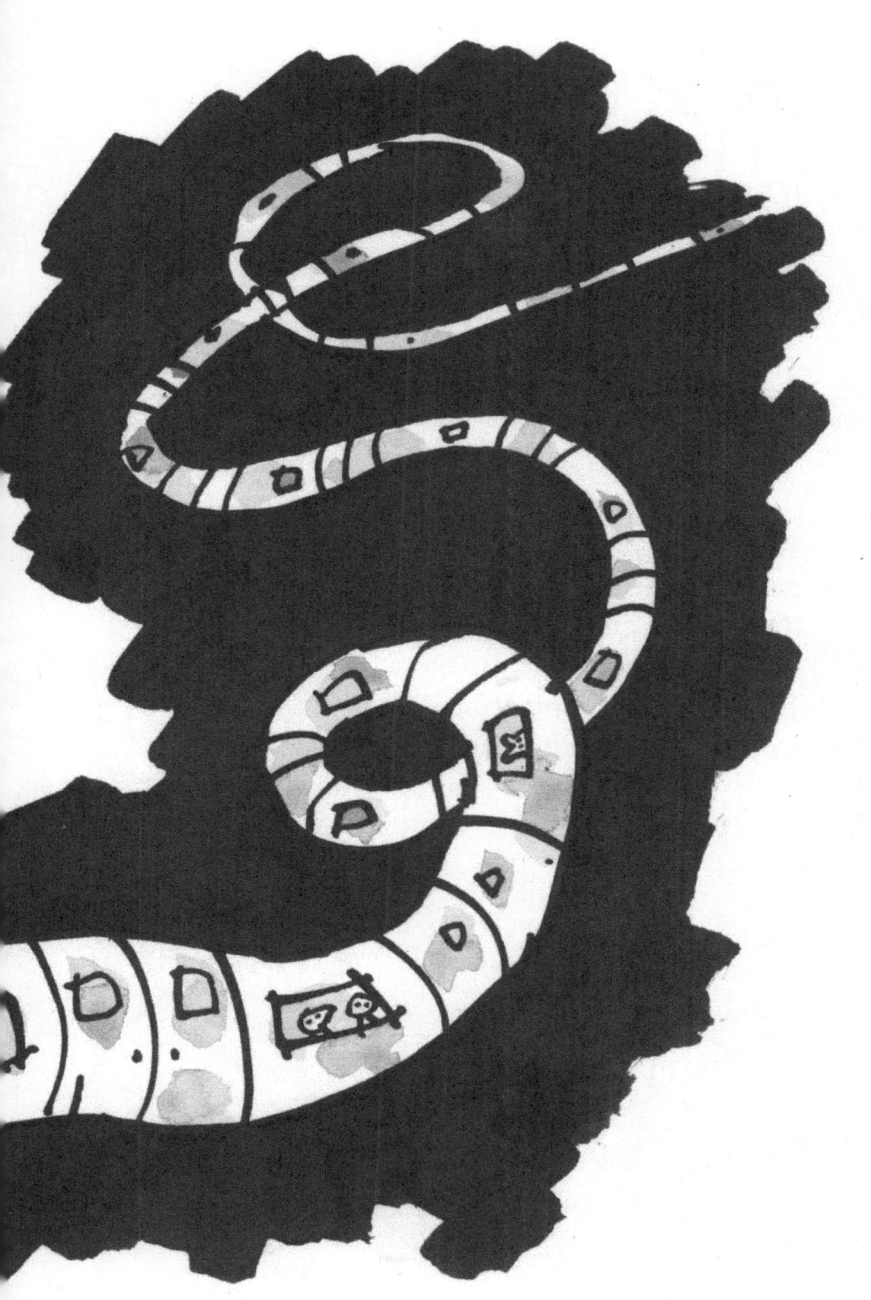

It's OK to Fail

It's OK to fail,
to fall flat and flop.
It's OK to start,
then stumble and... stop.

If you're finding tasks tricky
that's perfectly fine.
We can't all speed fast past the finishing line.

Don't stress in lessons, exams and tests
so long as you're trying your absolute best.
There's no need to panic,
the Earth will keep turning
if you tell yourself that
you're NOT failing...
                      but learning.

Book Meal

The blurb was the appetiser
The preface was the starter
The story was the main course
The epilogue was the afters

Chalk and Cheese*

Breakfast time, rusty nails
Toilet roll, humpback whales
Postage stamp, hairy ear
Muddy swamp, can of beer
Portuguese, heavy rocks
Totem pole, chicken pox
Violin, plastic bag
A to Z, oily rag
Football boot, buzzy bees

Cheese and chalk?
Chalk and cheese!

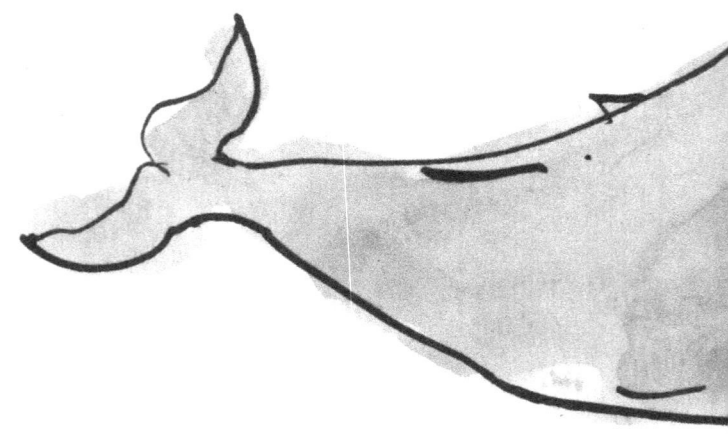

(*'Chalk and cheese' is an expression given to two people or things that have nothing in common)

Oscillating Ocelot

I'm an oscillating ocelot
I always oscillate a lot
Up from my bottom to my top
With feet fixed firmly on one spot
Move endlessly around the clock
Though feeling tired and fit to drop
I never, ever, ever stop
I try and try but I cannot

I'm an oscillating ocelot

Scrabble

I love playing Scrabble
There's no game that's better
Though I get frustrated
When a word's short of one lette

Pockets

Pockets are great for storing things
Tissues, tickets, coins, key rings

Gloves, bits of paper, five pound notes
Chewing gum, small stones, buttons for your coats

Handkerchiefs, shoelaces, sherbet dips
Wallets, phones, hair ties and hair clips

Chocolate, pens, pencils, shopping receipts
Apple cores, sunglasses, dog biscuit treats

And if your hands are feeling restless with nothing to do
Then put both of them in your pockets too

LostinSpace

Whostolemyspacebar?
It'sthekeyIreallyneed
Coswithoutitmypoetry's
Moredifficulttoread

Knock! Knock!

It's not the police knocking hard on your door,
it can't be a T Rex cos they are no more.
It isn't a postie delivering the post,
it's not Halloween and therefore not a ghost.

It's not Father Christmas (the wrong time
    of year),
it isn't a burglar so have no fear.
It isn't that neighbour you know all too well...

it's just the repair man who's mending
    your bell!

Rules?

My teacher always said that

a preposition isn't something to end
   a sentence with.
'And' must never start one.
Slang is a total no-no.
CaPital leTTeRs mUst Be usED apPrOpriatelY.
Hyphens should be placed between syllables.

But as a poet I say that

Rules are made to be
b-

       ro-

    ke-

 n

Dissimiles

He was hungry like a hat
As lazy as a lemon
Pompous like a pin
As monstrous as a melon

Cheeky like a chair
As queasy as a quetzal
Jealous like a germ
As puzzled as a pretzel

Timid like a tongue
As sensitive as slime
And silly like the similes
You're reading in this rhyme

Now can you create your own dissimiles?

Dangerous Fruit

A banana skin made me slip and trip,
I cracked a tooth on an orange pip.
Lemon juice squirted in my eye,
I sat on a pineapple and cried.

Watermelon + foot = broken bone,
I nearly choked swallowing a cherry stone.
An apple hurt my head falling from a tree,
yet you still insist fruit is good for me.

The Loooooooooongest Poem in the Universe

Welcome to the loooooooooongest poem
   in the Universe.
"But it's really short!" I hear you say.
Well, I've only just started writing it today....

Friendship Formula

You are my life's biggest +
We can never be ÷
Through the bad x
And the good x
Nobody is > you
We fit together like 2 ½s
Of the same π

Me − you = 0

Chop

I don't want a pork chop
or chicken leg instead.
I don't want a lamb kebab
or sausage in French bread.
I don't want a burger,
short back and sides will do.
But unfortunately I've come to
the wrong barber queue!

Limerick #1

A student of English, Delores
Completely consumed a thesaurus
She struggled for ages
But ate all the pages
And now her vocab is colossal, huge,
  gigantic, massive, vast, immense,
  prodigious, large, sizeable,
  extensive, considerable,
  enormous

Corners

In a corner of my room a spider spins its web
In my local corner shop I buy fresh milk
and bread
The sun shines brightly from a corner
of the sky
A teardrop falls from the corner of my eye

There's a corner of my shoe I can't fit
my toe in
There a corner of my garden which the roses
grow in
There are corners on triangles and rectangles
too
And a corner of my heart that's set aside
for you

oPOETician

```
H  F  Q  Z  L  A
C  S  X  N  U  I
G  M  V  J  K  B
P  O  E  T  R  Y
```

Butterflies

I've got butterflies in my stomach,
what should I do?
Rush to the hospital, the vet or the zoo?

Did caterpillars crawl inside me first?
With that unpleasant thought my discomfort
    grows worse.

They're flitting, flapping, fluttering about,
so I'm keeping my mouth open in the hope
    that...

they...

will...

fly...

OUT...

Fearless

I'm a fearless firefighter on the longest ladder,
a mountaineer streeeeeeetching to the top.
I'm a skilled acrobat entertaining a circus,
a parachutist not nervous to drop.

I'm a brave astronaut in a rip-roaring rocket,
a golden eagle poised ready to glide.
I'm a strong superhero soaring through blue skyways
when I'm playing on my

s
l
 i
  i
   i
    i
     i
      i
       i
        i
         i
          d
           e
            !

The Ghost Writer

"Teachers are aliens"
"Down with school"
"Jules luvs Jamie"
"Man U rool"

"Maths is mind-boggling"
"Odours smell"
"Eat your homework"
"I kan't spel"

"Me for Prime Minister"
"Poetry's cool"

Who scrawled graffiti
on our wall?

Sleepy Dog

Our dog won't sleep in the kitchen,
our dog won't sleep in the hall.
I lure her to the lounge with treats
but she won't sleep there at all

Our dog won't sleep on the landing,
it's a thing that she won't do.
A comfy cushion, sofa, chair,
she'll refuse each of them too.

Our dog won't sleep in her basket,
prefers somewhere else instead.
Cos though I tell her, "No, no, no!"
she will always choose my bed!

Lull

As a child
I was always asking myself
What's the scariest part of a storm?

The flickering, flashing lightning...

or the rumbling, roaring thunder?

Until I realised
what frightened me the most
was the uncertainty of the gap
between the two.

A Difficult Choice

The Hairy Hippos, Plastic Sofas
The Ice Pops, Tick Tick Boom!

Wild Wobbly Wellies, Yellow Yo-Yos
Men in Sheds, Goats Go Zoom

Two Tiny Teapots, PVA Glue
Sausages in the Sand

Can you please help and suggest a name
For our brilliant new rock band?

Holes

There's a hole in my pen that is leaking ink
A hole in my sock letting out a stink
A hole called a 'pouch' in a kangaroo
Two holes in my nose that I'm sniffing through

A hole in your thumb and it's oozing blood
A mole in the ground boring holes in mud
A hole in the leg of my sister's tights
A hole in my toast cos you took a bite

A hole in the 'o' that appears in 'more'
A worm drilling holes in my apple core
Holes in our eyes so our tears can drop
And my balloon has a hole so it's going to...

POP!

K 8 a B

O, o, o!
K 8 a b
U c, u c
K 8 a b
Y o y?
K 8 a b
999 - m r g n c!
K 8 a b 4 t

(PS: R u o k, K?)

Why not try to create a similar fun poem of your own?

On Finding an Acorn

From a tiny acorn massive oak trees grow
From the smallest raindrop winding rivers flow

Many quiet whispers may create a roar
Single violent actions might lead to a war

After gentle ripples wild tsunamis swell
Every human being starts as just a cell

From one speck of darkness sprang the Universe
From a tiny acorn I've produced this verse

Limerick #2

A woman who lived in Peru
Frequently felt déjà vu
A woman who lived in Peru
Frequently felt déjà vu
A woman who lived in Peru
Frequently felt déjà vu

If you don't know what 'déjà vu' is, look it up – or maybe you already have ;-)

Etc

Bus, lorry, cycle
Train, tram, car etcetera
Moon, planet, comet
Space, sun, star etcetera

Red, orange, yellow
Blue, green, brown etcetera
Place, city, village
Borough, town etcetera

Snow, thunder, lightning
Wind, hail, rain etcetera
So on and so forth
Same again etcetera

Woodpecker, Woodpecker

Woodpecker, woodpecker
Waking up the neighbourhood
Woodpecker, woodpecker
Feeling happy, feeling good
Woodpecker, woodpecker
Doing what woodpeckers should
Woodpecker, woodpecker
Peck-peck-peck-peck-peck-peck-peck
Peck-peck-peck-peck-peck-peck-peck
Peck-peck-peck-peck-peck-peck-peck

Pecking wood

Talk

When you have a bad day, can't cope any
 longer,
you're weak and you're wobbly, wish you
 were stronger,

when lying in bed is your choice recreation
until happiness is your poorest relation,

when you're feeling bruised, brittle, so close to
 breaking,
each step you're attempting's the toughest
 you're taking,

when your stomach's knotted, too tight
 to be undone…

then lighten that huge load by
 talking to someone.

Chopsticks

Soft noodles tangled up my hair
Egg fried rice spread across the chair
Crispy prawn balls rolled on the rug
Wontons plopped in Dad's coffee mug
Sweet and sour pork fell to the floor
Hot soy sauce decorated the door
The carpet was ruined by a chow mein stain
So I'm not gonna use chopsticks again

Pigs

High in the sky, far from the ground,
a creature made a snorting sound.
Its tail was curled, its snout was flat,
no bird I knew looked quite like that.

It had four trotters, skin pale pink.
This caused me to reflect and think
what people say must be a lie...

There is no doubt that pigs CAN fly!

Tiping

The quack brownb foxx
Lunmps over the lazy doe

Kevin only star ted ttiping
Seven dayys ago

"The quick brown fox jumps over the lazy dog" is a **pangram** – a very short sentence containing all the letters of the alphabet at least once. It is used to teach people to type. Can you write your own pangram?

Shape Poem

Our teacher said,
"Please write a shape poem."
(That's a poem in the shape of its subject.)

So after thinking about it...
and thinking about it...
I wrote this –
a poem-shaped shape poem.

Whodunnit?

The detectives arrived at the scene of the crime...

Victim A: mesmerised by dazzling rhyme
Victim B: developed a reading infatuation
Victim C: grew a fantastic imagination
Victim D: heard rhythms racing round her head
Victim E: swapped his TV for some books
  instead

And who was the culprit wanted by the police force?
I'm sure that *you* know

it was the poet of course!

Cupboard Under the Stairs

Shopping bags, cardboard boxes
Dog food tins, plastic welly
Brushes, brooms, vacuum cleaner
Rusty clock, something smelly

Ironing board, washing basket
Dusty books, busted heaters
Toilet rolls, metal bucket
Pot of glue, power meters

Photo frame, bits of carpet
Litter bin, broken chairs
And ME playing hide 'n seek
In the cupboard under the stairs

Birthday

I wrote this poem
as a very special present
from me to you.

I hid it in this book
so you wouldn't find it.
Though you obviously have
so it's not a surprise 😔

But I hope you enjoy it anyway...

HAPPY BIRTHDAY!!!

Bugged

A grumpy minibeast protested,
"I think my name's absurd.
I'm no lady, I'm a gent
and an insect, not a bird!"

Henry's Wives

Catherine of Aragon: Messy divorce
Anne Boleyn: Beheaded, of course
Jane Seymour: Prematurely passed
Anne of Cleves: Divorced – real fast
Catherine Howard: Another execution
But Catherine Parr: Perfect solution!*

*Henry VIII died while they were still married, so she outlived him.

How Long is a Poem?

It can be:

as long as a child's widest smile
as long as the teeth on a crocodile
as long as the Eiffel Tower is tall
as long as your nose (and that's not long at all)
as long as my sister's ponytail
as long as a snail's slimy trail
as long as a queue at a bus stop
as long as a sausage from the butcher's shop
as long as a hundred anaconda snakes
cos a poem can be as long as it...
as long as it...
      as long as it...
           as long as it...
                takes

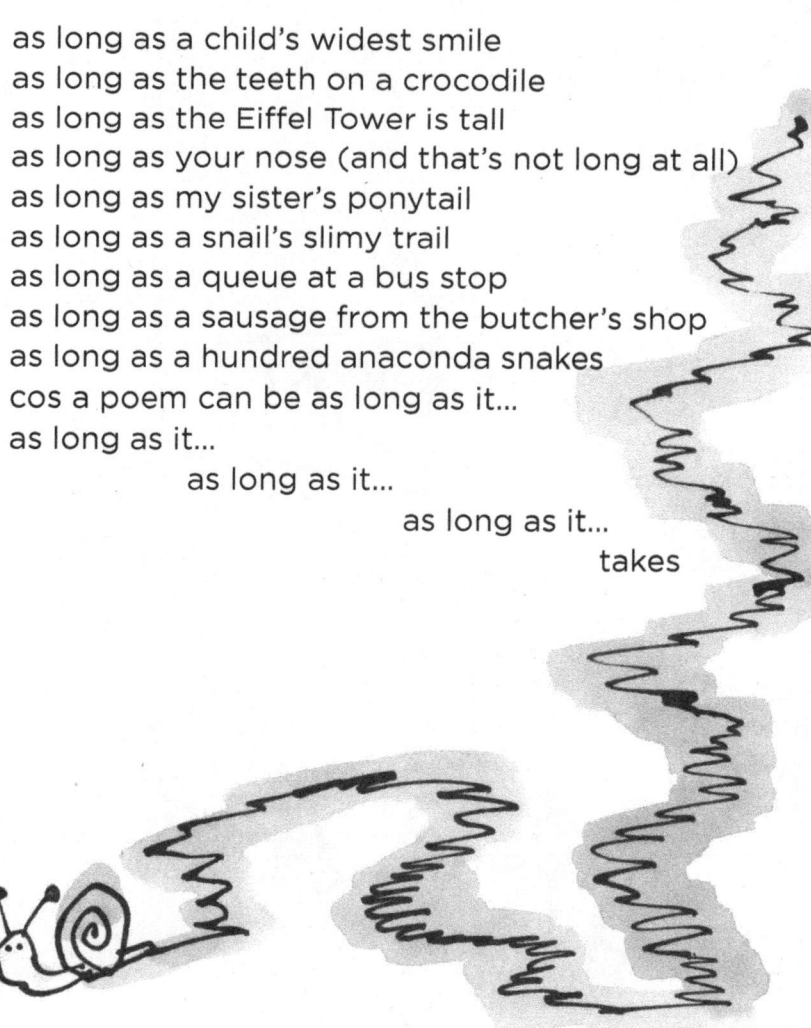

N Vwls

T hlp th nvrnmnt dn't y thnk
W shld stp sng vwls nd sv mr nk?
t's nt s crzy s sm mght sy
Bcs y cn stll rd ths nywy

Fastly?

You could **rapidly** run an Olympic race,
disappear **quickly** without a trace,
promptly pack your bags for holiday,
speedily gobble up a takeaway,

be **swiftly** blown over in a strong gale,
even slide **slowly** like a slug or a snail.
But you could never fly ***fastly*** like a plane or
 a bird

because ***fastly*** definitely isn't a word!

Although, as the poem states, "fastly" isn't a word,
I hear it many times in class during my poetry writing
lessons. "Fast" is the correct word to use instead.

Magical

Dressed in a smart suit of silver and black,
he produced twenty rabbits out of his hat,
sawed a man and a woman in half
as the audience shrieked!
As the audience gasped!

While waving his magic wand around
he levitated high above the ground,
pulled ten silk scarves from each of his ears,
yelled "Abracadabra!"
And – in a flash –

disappeared!

It's eating in-between times,
it's neither here nor there,
a meal enjoyed mid-morning
and one that's best to share.

It's too late for your breakfast,
it's too soon for your lunch.
So maybe at eleven
we all can grab some

Brunch!

Sky

The sky's above us in the air
We are down here while it's up there

The sky is high, it's never low
It's full of clouds that come and go

It holds the sun, the stars, the moon
Kites, aeroplanes, rockets, balloons

And birds and flying insects too
The Earth's blanket of brilliant blue

It can be orange, also red
When inky black it's time for bed

If weather's wet it's gloomy grey
I hope...
         the sky...

                won't float...

                       away...

When days are too long
and my head's in a spin,
whatever I do
there's no way I can win.
When problems are piled high
in mountains so steep,
I turn off the light,
shut my eyes tight and...

Zzzzzzzz

Limerick #3

There was an old lady from Hull
And she bumped into a bull
The bull said "Ow!"
Crashed into a cow
Then the cow smashed into the wall

This is the first poem I ever wrote, aged 6.

Sorted!

If things don't go here
If things don't go there
If they don't really seem to go
anywhere
No need to worry
Stress, fret or fuss
Just file them under M
For Miscellaneous

Finally?

If this poem is the first you've found
You're probably reading this book
The wrong way round!

About the Poet and the Illustrator

NEAL ZETTER began writing poetry when he was six years old. Since 1994 he has staged his fun poetry-writing workshops and performances in hundreds of schools and libraries in the UK and beyond, teaching 3-103 year olds to create their own fantastic poetry.

He has won the Silver Book Award, been acclaimed by the Reading Agency and Book Trust, had poems on London's buses, in the Guardian newspaper and in many anthologies. He has performed his adult poems on radio, in the Royal Festival Hall, at a League 2 football match, festivals, weddings and funerals (really), countless top West End Comedy clubs and hosted his own club for ten years. This is Neal's third book for Otter-Barry Books, following *The Universal Zoo* and *The Shape of Rainbows*. For all things Neal see **cccpworkshops.co.uk**

WILL HUGHES is an illustrator of children's books from Malvern in Worcestershire. After a Foundation year at Hereford College of Arts he took a degree in Illustration at the University of Edinburgh.

He mainly works in ink and watercolour because he likes how that lends itself to quick and lively illustrations with character and humour. In 2019 Will was part of the Picture Hooks Mentoring Scheme, which culminated in two pieces of his work being exhibited at the Scottish National Gallery of Modern Art. He has illustrated six published books including *The Universal Zoo* and *The Shape of Rainbows* by Neal Zetter, and he enjoys running workshops for children on drawing and storytelling. He lives in London.